I0410464

My Thoughts My Views

One Race Understanding Another

By Renda Wilson

Copyright © 2016 The Underground Railroad Book Publishing

All rights reserved.

Table of Contents

"Life's journey as a free moral agent and the Creator's expectation for ALL is to speak the truth." – Renda Wilson

I grew up in Boston, Mass and relocated to AL in 2005. Writing is part of my life. Writing helps to ease my spirit. I am a proud mother of two. I am best known for caring for and helping children in my community. I am the founder of Helping Hands Children's Center, a non-profit organization in Birmingham, AL. This organization has allowed me to see the down side of our communities and to analyze the impact it has on families. Through this organization I am able to have a positive impact on our future generations.

My Thoughts and My Views of our past and present connection to the CREATOR is a Message concerning Nation understanding Nation.

Chapter 1

Colored Difference

What makes us different is on the outside but inside we are all the same. "Two Races" Do we share the same laws, as a woman of color, I want to say we share the same laws but the truth is Realistically we do not there's laws that only apply to minority's and laws that applies to the white race, same laws but treated differently when comes to color and status 80% of the time our court system stands in the corner of those who's financially stable like how much money you have and being able to obtain good attorney. Having a good attorney, you have a greater chance of winning most white people think because of their skin color they can just walk into a court room and beat any case that's not true in fact poor whites are on the same level as black people, notice how I did not say poor colored people because in this society black people are all the same it does not matter if we are rich, poor our status remains the same "Colored."

The white race according to society there is a difference a poor white person will not get the same treatment as a white person with money. We can fight each other every day on who is the better race, first we must try understand the anger the frustration of the black race our vision how we both really have so much in common how we survive, how we live but we do treat differently and it shows we bleed red but our skin is what's different and has cause so much confusion.

Why is color such a big deal? Color was a gift from our creator, both races have some form of unique and special quality about themselves. When I see another race I see "Creation" but what make creation so ugly is laws, status, and one race feeling like their better than another race. Because of this kind of thinking it has been a battle of the two races for generations.

Because of this generational curse we have made it a point to let each other no how we really feel about each other and we do it through hate, using violence, and training our children to hate. I am not pointing the finger that's not what this is about, but both races colored and white, poor and rich are descendants of a long line of an ugly history of slavery! Yes I said it, and I can because saying slavery does not affect me because I have learned to understand my past. I have forgiven those that robed me of my heritage and my history. I can't turn back time, all I can do for myself, and my family, is to teach them what was taken from us and walk through this journey of life with respect and knowing who I am, and in history, where I came from. I know who my ancestors were before they were robbed of their humanity.

Chapter 2

<u>America Past vs Present</u>

We all have to truly forgive our past in order to move forward in our future as we grow further and further away from this ugly history, one of worlds darkest secrets that nobody wants to talk about "slavery". We all want to wave good bye to slavery without both races, truly healing from it. Our communities are getting worse each day not only the Black Communities, it's also effecting the white communities because you cannot hide the truth for long. Interracial relationships are growing and we must remember the children are a mixture of both races, and we all know they are the seed of their father.

White woman, are more in interracial relationships with other races, more than white men, so interracial children will gravitate more to their father's race allowing them to experience some of society's negativity and racist ways from both sides. This will become very confusing to them because their part of the two races, so that's why it is important to teach history in the school system to the children in both communities white and colored because if we don't, what our children experience in society will surely teach them to continue the cycle of hatred.

My thoughts, on how we can fix the problem and what tools to use oh, yes there are ways just like our oppressors controlled the minds of our ancestors, we have to take our communities back. In doing this it will take teaching, learning and getting the attention of the young ones. We must first give them back their lost identity. While fixing the problems, we also need to help the white race to understand and show them why it's so important for the black youth to learn who they are as a people.

We also need the white race to help with teaching as well in schools, daycare centers, and afterschool programs these teaching needs to start at an early age so that we will produce a proud generation of youth.

We also need to teach each other's history, the correct history, because I know European history was not all good. Some of them were slaves also. Having a clear understanding of our past will help us both black and white understand why poor whites wanted to leave their home land and move to a faraway land escaping poverty. They used some of the bible laws to colonize a land and become a successful race of people. This is something they probably could have never bone if they had remained in their own home land. It's not too late to open old books, we need to learn this history also.

Learning the teachings about the colored race and where we started from the beginning, learning our native tongues, learning our native foods, learning our culture and most of all knowing our strength and how we survived for generations and we're still standing means we are a great nation and a powerful race. We were born to survive. Our ancestors prayed for us, they knew it was over for them. They were never given a fair chance but they wanted us, their descendants, the future generations, to be free. We must never forget our past or what they went through for us to be free!

Our ancestors became free in death. They raised boys to men and girls to become women. Our ancestors taught girls to be young ladies, to become a helpmate to their husbands and keepers of our communities. Also to raise their children with morals and respect to continue the journey to freedom.

Chapter 3

Sense of Direction

Knowledge is power and power is strength, to not know who you are or where you come from is lost history. To hide history from our children will allow them to become zombies in the world walking with no direction.

We need to build strong, powerful men and women. We have become commercial puppets only knowing how to keep up with fashion and learning how to sell fashion for the designers. We have become walking manikins selling their designs as commercial puppets! This type of teaching has to stop. There's nothing wrong with fashion or living good but it is a problem when that's all we have to offer.

Let's teach our children that they are more than just a fashion statement. if we continue in the same direction our race will forever be lost from a lack of knowledge.

More and more prisons are being built. In time the colored races will be no more. The truth is our past will be written off, only the strong will survive and the weak will die. We don't have time for foolishness any more. Let's repair our communities, remove the negative obstacle and jealousness from our hearts so that our race can come together as a community and grow into a village.

If we really believe we're equal to other races well think again. It is going to take changing our thought process, learning true history, and changing our attitudes. Doing all of this will not make us the same as others but separate ourselves from others. Even a dog is worried about our next move.

Power is knowledge until we come together and stop being fool's and lovers of foolishness, destroying our communities, not becoming the people our ancestors prayed for us to become. We will never be equal to no one or nothing.

Truth is, so a man thinks so shell he be. Your thoughts can destroy your motivation, thinking is one thing, and doing is another there is a difference. Motivation is the key to real success. Losing our way has been an ongoing problem. We would rather put our hands straight into the fire not thinking of the after affect. We like to feel the heat first instead of learning that fire will burn. No one should know your next move, our ancestors did not live like this. We're an insult to them if only they could see us now what would they say? This is something to meditate on.

Chapter 4

Freedom and Education

Fighting for freedom was for us to be able to utilize our rights. So many of us fought whites and colored people for us to have the right to live free. The chains are off. We are not in physical bondage anymore, we are in mental bondage, and it's our fault.

Men and woman suffered by the hand of wicked people for freedom. Not every white person is wicked. Lots of white men and woman fought for our freedom also.

Let's take the time to learn first before we place every white person in the same category. Respect is given not taken. We can demand respect but why should anyone give us respect when in fact we don't even respect each other. Once we learn to respect ourselves and our communities then we will truly be able to experience freedom. Loving who we are as colored people should mean more to us. We need to learn how our people before us worked and supported each other. They had no choice see, freedom allows us to have choices.

Looking back at history then we are an ungrateful generation. The problem is we have not acknowledged or respected those before us, the fighters. The ones who died for us to have the right in expressing what we like or dislike. The right to live in certain communities, to walk into department stores, yes some might say my money spends like their money. Well if we did not have real fighters before us you would not be able to spend your money where they spend theirs.

Learning European history was a down fall for our people. We need to see the truth about us, the colored race. It's so sad because we have to learn the deepest levels of our history in collage. What's wrong with learning black history in elementary school? If our children learn early then we will see a race with love for themselves and for their community.

Did anyone ever stop to think that hiding the truth from colored people has made them uncaring? They don't see many colored professionals and if they do it's what someone else is pleased with. They don't hear about black history, I mean the real black history. In schools white children are proud of their European heritage their taught about those who paved the way for them. Our children don't have the same teachings. If we start this teaching then we would not have black children running around like fashion bill boards with an identity crisis.

Maybe we would not have children being held up at gun point. Without education we will continue to use material things to lift us up. This is another reason why our communities are in danger. The have's and have nots in the urban community is death to the ones that have a little more than the next person. We are not free in our own communities. This is a product of identity crisis.

Daylight

Daylight allows mankind to move on earth

Darkness calms us down

There's a time to rest and a time to move

Flowers cannot bloom without water and sun

Just like mankind cannot grow without spiritual

Wisdom and knowledge

Allowing the Creator to manifest HIS work in our souls

So that mankind would live life like heaven is here on earth

Our paths and blessings are ordained

Darkness can hinder the vision

Light will restore it

Chapter 5

History and Traditions

There is a real problem with keeping someone else's traditions and not educating ourselves by learning our own traditions. It's very important to become knowledgeable about our own traditions. Being together on one accord teaches us and allows us to understand and respect our neighbors and their beliefs. We don't have to believe in what they believe but we do have to respect their beliefs.

If our oppressors only knew removing people from their homeland to another land far across the waters how could they escape?

Our people were captured and put into bondage not knowing this strange land. Running away could have been an option and if it was an option really how far could they have gone? So not allowing them to keep what was most important to them, their culture, allowing them to remain grounded in their own traditions would have made America's colored youths grounded and respectful. Because this is part of our problem our whole culture and history was removed from us. We became lost not knowing who we were and our youth have become one of America's most talked about nightmare.

Not allowing us to keep our past alive for future generations being able to pass it down generation to generation was very unhuman. But allowing us to keep someone else's history, traditions, and cultures has made us solely dependent on others like the US government. We must become self-sufficient. We have become comfortable in an uncomfortable situation and it has been this way for a long time generation after generation the cycle of oppressed, depressed people.

It's time to wake up! Time waits for no one. We have taught and continued with the teachings of our oppressors. We passed their teachings down to our children. Our children are confused and lost. America is in deep trouble because we will have a lost generation with nothing to lose and nothing to care about. This type of mindset is dangerous to all of us black and white.

Allowing our history to be taught in schools early plus having a separate class for black history so that our children can be taught correctly. We should not sugar cote it or water it down. We must give it to them the way it happened. I mean give them everything. This will be the start of understanding and the start of unifying, healing and releasing the pain that has been held inside for decades from our oppressors.

Although change is good we can never change the fact that we come from a back ground of tribes that were a people with gut instinct. Tribal people will always have those ways even if they don't know that they are descendants of a tribe.

It's in their blood their soul their spirits speak to them that's why we have police officers expressing fear of the colored man it's because they understand and they know what the black man is made of they no his roots his history but that colored man just doesn't know who he is or his strength.

It's just like a child being born without a father. That child does not know the fathers side and most grow up not ever knowing. The mother sees so much of that man in her child and the child grows up just like someone he or she never knew.

Having us learn the ways of our oppressor has cost us many lives, especially our youth because there down for whatever.

Chapter 6

Identity Crises

Our youth don't have a since of direction. Learning the ways of our oppressor is all we know: how he speaks, how he thinks, what he eats, how he lives, how he treats his children, how he interacts with authority. Everything he does we follow. He has shown us so much about himself some of us think we can just be him.

 We have a serious identity crisis. We need to reeducate ourselves and redirect the teaching that was taught to us, because once we as people of color start acting in the ways of the white race they will remind us who we really are quickly. No disrespect intended but this is a fact.

We must understand being taught is one thing, and acting it out is different. We must know why it's very important to learn who we really are, educate ourselves and learn to love each other enough to pull the next colored person up. We need to stop thinking everyone else owes us, they owe us nothing. We have to do for ourselves.

We always depend on others to help us with our children. It's time we help ourselves. It's up to us. Some of our black leaders made it by stealing from us and the community's using nonprofit organizations and getting grant money, while very little of the funding goes into the community. Some of our people make it out becoming a success story for our youth to admire but very few bring their success back to the community.

We as people of color have failed our communities. We have allowed our children and our communities to become dependent on the outside world to help us. Our communities should educate their own children in every area. This will make an impact for the future generation.

 A race of people that was once controlled for so long, being set free without being educated on how to be free, has caused our people to become uncaring, selfish, and disrespectful. It's so sad because the white race doesn't understand the importance of educating our children correctly with the correct history.

 Our society does not want to teach the real history concerning the colored race because it's an ugly topic. It saddens them to hear what was created by the hands of their forefathers.

So to teach us that ugly history will open up old wounds that has healed for them but not us. To open those old covered up scares will make them apologize every chance they get. Its ok we understand it was not you, so no blame is pointed towards you, "on behalf of colored people, from me to you Apology accepted." To you our oppressor's descendants, I can hear you even if you don't want to discuss the ugly history that has a hold on our people. If you say that was in the past just let it stay in the past, I feel your sorrow and your pain. Who would really want to be part of an ugly history that tortured another race. I understand why the white race continue to say that's the past.

But understand that the past has haunted colored people for generations. Our children don't know about their history and this is due to our society keeping a part of history out of our education system. Should it continue to stay out of our history books? When our children look in those books they don't see themselves. Hate is not the answer but understanding and learning is the key to a brighter future for both races black and white. We need to successfully close that ugly chapter in history and make it better for all our future generations to understand the past, in order to fully release it but never forget it, learn it, and embrace it. Remembering the past for colored people plays a big role in our current situation. As colored people we have to fight harder in life to gain success more than any other race. Believe me it's not easy being a colored person, it's a gift.

Chapter 7

Community Building

In our communities we have outsiders coming in opening up community organization for our youth. These ordinary average community organization are offering programs that teach nothing of value. They are managed by white people that are getting most of the grants that bring these organizations in our communities that do not help our children with what they really need.

 Helping them to become productive, self-sufficient adults is not the intention of these organizations. Nothing from nothing leaves nothing, and that's what our children are getting from these programs, nothing. How is this still happening? Churches are a big business in our communities. We are being used in our own communities. They give a little and they take a lot, gaining big in our communities. In 5 to 6 years after doing business with our children they close down because they have made it so big there able to retire early. While maybe 1 or 2 of our youth became a success story from their program, a very low number with their programs actually are a benefit to our children.

Black children don't learn like white children. The educational tools given to our children don't help. We as colored people can become a better people it's in us, but it's up to us, as colored people to teach our own children. We have the tools, all it takes is for us to open our own nonprofit organizations in our own communities. Let's take our children to the next level of what life has to offer them. We all can learn from this. We can make changes but we have to grab our babies and stop allowing greed to keep us in bondage. They are free born and we should always teach them that so they are not blown away by every wind and doctoring.

Just because someone opens up something in our community and pass out food and clothes does not mean your gaining anything! It just means that our children are being labeled by society. It means that we need what their giving us but to them it means we cannot do anything on our own. WAKE UP my people this is serious. We need to educate ourselves and understand what's really going on in our communities and take them back.

Chapter 8

<u>Darkness to Light</u>

When I look in the mirror I see a long history of strong black woman who struggle to live and survive. I walk like them. I move like them. I work like them but I am free.

 Free from all darkness, light is over me and I struggle to keep darkness out of my life. Knowing who I am means more to me than anything in this world because it sets me apart spiritualty, mentally, and emotionally.

I love my life. I may not have everything but I am educated with self-respect. I can walk into a warm house in the winter months and in the summer I can walk into a cool home. I have clothes on my back and shoes on my feet. I can watch television when I want to. I have a means of communication so I can talk to family members in another state. I don't need a day set aside to visit my folks and to be told what time to come back. I have full control over my ever day life and I worked hard for it. I am free. I am a free decedent of slaves.

I made my way. I understand who I am. I understand where I came from. I understand what it takes to maintain. I know how to respect others and I also know how to get respect.

I taught my children the values of being free and respecting others. Loving our neighbors as we love ourselves. I don't allow anyone to cloud my thinking or tell me what is right or what is wrong.

I was not born this way. I learned it. I educated myself. I read a lot European and black history. I taught myself. I stared to gather information. I learned what the generations before my grandmother stood for and how they were brought down by another race. How they struggled to keep what little bit they could of their own history and culture. How they held on and past down whatever little bit they knew.

I can go back 4 generations. 95 percent of black people do not even know 2 generations of important things like family's name, what tribe they were from, their native tongues, their foods, and the list goes on and on. It was not permitted on the plantations. They were given a whole new identity and at some point they just gave up.

They did not mean anything to anyone. How do you live like that, you don't. You just survive. Most of what our ancestors, because of a lack of strength, just gave up. They could not do it anymore. They had to deal with so much like their children being taken away, witnessing beatings, hangings, and people being treated worse than animals. If you remove an animal from the group they will become depressed and lonely. Our ancestors became depressed. They lived for their oppressor and not for themselves.

Generation after generation lived for others. Our ancestors were not able to care for their families. All they knew taking care of others.

Sound familiar? We as colored people do not take care of our own. We don't even do business with our own people. We would rather do business with others. We were taught not to mingle with each other, with our own people.

Our oppressor feared any type of relationship that would form between the slaves. This teaching has been passed down. That's why we have so much black on black crime and black on black hate.

The Ruler of Creation

As the oceans strongest waves passes by

It takes away the breath from the deepest of the bottom

It calms the sea world while showing mankind

Who is in charge

The waves re-build the sea world with a new look

Respect and NEVER underestimate the ruler of Creation

Chapter 9

<u>Self-Destruction</u>

Our youth don't even know how to respect or love each other. Somehow we stopped being a community. Although our ancestors were deprived of socializing with their own people they respected and loved their people. They helped each other even if they had to do it in secret.

We are free but we live like slaves in our own captivity. We continue to live on the plantations. The only difference is we get paid for doing nothing, while our ancestors had to work the plantations daily just to receive the pickings from hogs to feed their families.

They made it through all work and no play. They filled their stomachs with whatever was left over from there oppressors table to survive. Survival was their mission. I don't know why because at the end of their road was death.

Today's generation kill, steal, and rape each other daily on the plantation. That's why we have to be policed every minute and hour of the day. It has not registered in our youth's mind why black lives don't matter. Black lives don't even matter to us.

Once we start teaching our youth why they are being watched every minute of the hour, and start teaching them at the age of 5 years old or even in the womb, planting that seed while nurturing the belly, that baby will enter into this world with a nurturing soul.

Teaching our young ones who they really are is important. They need to know they come from a strong race of people that have a long line of greatness. We must keep watering the seeds daily and watching them grow and blossom with respect, so that they will respect others.

Who do we blame? We can't blame society any more. Our growth and learning in this day starts at home or should start at home. It's unfortunate that not only our children need teaching, the leadership of the home also needs to be taught as well.

Most of our children come from single family homes and this can be a problem. It just depends on who is leading the home, man or woman, strong or weak. We know a weak person cannot teach. They allow any and every thing to go on. They have no will power. They have no control and they don't know how to control.

If the weak person is a woman, her down fall is her man. She moves when he says move. Everything she does is according to the sound of his command so her children are surrounded by a weak mother and a man that is abusive. Sometimes the man is not only abusive to their mother but to her children also and she allows the abuse.

Chapter 10

<u>A Weak or Strong household</u>

A strong woman doesn't allow her children to take over. She's totally in control of her everyday life and her household. She is not looking for someone to tell her that she's doing a good job. She knows she's doing her best. Her top priority is caring for her household, so she handles her business. She's a fighter. She's marriage material. She is the kind of woman that holds her man or husband down, showing him daily she has his back and allowing him to be a man.

She raises boys to be men and daughters to be woman. She works very hard to keep her children away from corruption. She works hard to live in a safe community even if it means to move in a neighborhood with very little income. She does not care because everything she does is for her family. She maintains and keep her home a home. Her first love is spiritual and her next is her family. Her love is so strong for her family. She does whatever it takes to protect them.

A weak Man has no knowledge of who he is. He does not know his self-worth. He's looking for a mother figure more than a father figure. He is a man that was raised by a weak woman. He grows up very fast helping to support his mother and siblings. He becomes the man of the household. He has to protect his mother from a weak man.

He starts to have children early. He picks the same kind of women that raised him. As a father he's now experiencing the baby momma drama from a woman he's chosen to have kids with. She turns him into a weaker man under her control.

He has no way out of this circle so he become depressed, and stressed with no to turn to. At times he does not want a way out. He is caught up on being controlled. It makes him feel loved.

Growing up with a weak mother he becomes attracted to women that are weak and more controlling. He was never taught or shown anything other than how to survive only knowing poverty, struggling and of course weakness. He turns to the streets and the streets teach him. He learns how to make money selling drugs. He learns how to become a man from the streets. He starts to surround himself with those that think like him and they become his street family.

He is not learning anything positive because in the streets there is nothing positive to learn.

Connecting himself with gangs, and having more children from the same type of weak women, the cycle continue until he surrounds himself with positive people. He has to let that old life go and that's hard for him to. When he finds a strong positive woman, he takes her through the ringer. She is what he needs, but he does not understand she is his rib.

She's too positive for him. He's not use to this type of woman. He starts to live a double life having side woman. His main woman is at home waiting on him daily. She doesn't hang in the streets. She doesn't go out to clubs. She's a home body. She stands by her man until he gets caught up.

This type of man is what our prisons systems ends up with. He is another colored man headed for self-destruction.

A strong man is one that cares for his family. He's a man that was raised by a strong woman. He completes every mission he sets out for. He takes time out with his children. He chooses a wife like his mother, a strong woman. If things don't work out, he understands and respects the decision made between him and his wife. He will always care for his family. For the sake of their children he knows how to co-parent. He's a business man. He loves a positive strong woman. His mother is his number one lady.

He's gentle and supportive. He was taught right and he will not allow any one in his circle that he does not feel comfortable with. He is a private person and does not socialize with just any one. He's on a higher level and is very spiritual. Momma taught him well, and he does not give up so easy. He's a go getter, this type of man is a one man show. He does not need the streets to teach him anything.

Most of our grandparents are long gone. They were the keepers of our families. They kept us all together and in line. They put us in place when we stepped out of line. They were our parents. I believe our grandparents not being here anymore is death to us all.

Most of us can't move and don't know what to do without grandma and grandpa. Through our ups and downs they are missed so much. We're walking around like lost puppies without our grandparents.

Grandma's house was our second home. When we got pregnant grandmas was the place to be. When a baby was being born we took that baby straight to grandma's house after being released from the hospital. We all depended on our grandparents. They had our backs, especially grandma.

Grandparents in this generation are between the ages of 29-41. They know nothing about being grandparents. They are still learning how to be parents. How can you be happy about becoming a grandparent so early? I know things happen but if you're doing the same things as your child like partying, getting high, and having a house full of friends, you're not a grandparent. You're a parent with grandchildren, a support of whatever your children do.

A real grandparent will teach the child and would not support foolishness. Look at the difference. A child will hide foolishness from grandma because grandma don't play. She expects more out of her grandchildren. Her dreams of her grandchildren becoming something are very high.

Grandma has secrets from her past. She will go to her grave with them before she makes a fool of herself. You will never no or understand why grandma looked old at a young age. Just know she was full of wisdom. She understands life. She knows how to respect herself and others. She also knew how to speak out if need be.

Chapter 11

<u>Lost Generation</u>

Grandma loved her family she was the last of our past. She was borne free but it did not feel like it to her. She worked hard, she was a strong woman. She was a survivor, her whole life grandma wanted her children and her grandchildren to show the world where we came from. Grandma would all ways set her grandchildren down and tell the stories that her mother told her. We are missing a big part of our live today, our grandparents.

History is what keeps us grounded. It helped us in understanding who we were and where we came from. Hear the cries of our ancestors, don't let their suffering be in vain. We have to be their voices, there keepers of the history. They wanted us to keep and teach our children. Teaching our children will build successful lives in this land. Never forget your past.

 Love never hate, give and never expect anything back from anyone. Love life, and respect others, white and colored. We are two different races created by one creator. There are hidden graves with a race of people crying out. Don't let the struggle be in vain. They are our ancestors we never knew. We look like them, we walk like them. They are in us and we are in them. Once we learn about them we will see greatness in our lives and our children lives.

Stop running because there is nowhere to run. Listen to their cries. They bared the pain so we could be free. Use your freedom wisely with wisdom and turn darkness into light.

We are a lost generation today with no real community leaders, and broken homes. Most of our children are in the system. State agencies are placing our children in homes with no real counseling. These are our future generations, future doctors, lawyers, and government workers. Without the proper counseling and treatments for these children we will be in trouble. Without these services they will not be fit to take care of themselves let alone our country.

Our children are ticking time bombs just waiting for the right time to go off. Our law enforcement are in a position where they are not taking any chances. Most of our law enforcement feel like they have to do what they have to do in order to prevent themselves from becoming victims. Gun violence is on the rise. 95 percent of American households have a firearm. Citizens are taking down criminals daily. Most of us are tired of being victims.

Chapter 12

<u>Who is Raising our Children?</u>

State agencies wants to raise our children and with that being said we are up against the biggest fight ever. They are not helping the problem. They are just creating a bigger mess for law enforcement to handle. Then the police get blamed for handling a destructive child that the parents can't reach for whatever reason. The state agency failed them.

We need to take our children back. We are in a time were children have become the parents. Parents are wondering what just happened and how did it happen?

Where do we go from here? Well that's the million-dollar question. I think children get away with so much in this day and age they have no idea about being punished.

If I tell my child what to do, he or she should not think its ok to call law enforcement on me. That's a problem. Besides the police have so many other issues to deal with. I can almost guess the local police department would rather see children be corrected by their parents, because they have no tolerance for disrespectful adults. Let alone having to deal with a disrespectful child.

The state agencies have placed the burden on everyone else while they just keep removing children from their homes. This is an epidemic and needs to stop.

Reunifying children back with their parents with counseling will stop the continuous of removing children from their homes.

Failing our children will become another one of America's nightmares. Our children need us more than anything. They are hurting and crying out for help. We have more children in foster care than any other country. American's nightmare is a lost generation of poor white and colored children. Everything has been stripped from them at an early age. They are angry and in a defensive mood, not trusting anyone. They are moving from house to house because no one knows how to deal with them.

It's like being incarcerated. Most of their lives they have been in custody with the state for so long they don't know how to live like a normal child. Social workers are burned out there trained to not show emotions. It becomes easy to remove children from their parents. It's a real job. Human lives have been taken to another level in our society. What has our country become?

Young girls and boys are placed together in group homes. Sexual activities runs ramped in there so our children turn to what makes them feel good "Sex" and "Drugs" numbing the pain.

Most of the time children go into a loving and caring home. When things are not going their way they become a threat to the household and make like difficult for the foster parents. The state agency will trust that child's word over the foster parents, because most of the children in foster care have learned early how to be manipulators. The whole dam program has become a big money making business. It's unreal most of these children will soon be mothers and fathers. The cycle will continue without counseling. This will lead to another generational curse. It seems like an unstoppable situation. If a child is removed from their home with no communication or family ties we will have a lost generation just like slaves. It is the same concept, there is no difference.

Emergency disaster, America, disaster signs social, economic, political, and most of all race.

We are hurting ourselves, no more peace. We are living in prophecy that ur Creator spoke of throughout the Bible.

Communities use to raise children to respect authority. Child protective services was not in high demand because children were raised by families: aunt, uncle, or grandparents. Our children need us now more than ever.

Who do we blame for this mess up? Well I would say the parents are to blame. Most parents became a product of their environment. Stressed out and depressed, allowing themselves to be put in a state of hopelessness. They end up not caring about anyone but themselves. Healing their pain with drugs and alcohol, becoming friends with their addictions. They are letting down the ones that need them and love them. No matter what condition they chose to live in, their children craves the love of their presents. They would fight to stay with them no matter what. A child's love for their parents is unconditional. So we cannot point fingers. There is really no one to blame. Child protective services is doing their job, and the parents have deep scares that their hiding within never healing. Also not owning up to their faults, this is their generational curse.

As time goes on we will have more children in foster homes. This is due to the lack of services for our children and a lack of trust. Not much is done to help their immediate situation.

Being in foster care for these children become survival. When a foster child is placed in a home the foster parent has to go through so much. The foster child is placed in a home with so many issues and the deepest and most remembered is being torn apart from their parents. Because of that horrible moment in their little lives they put up a defense and hatred towards adults. Their concept is that every adult is the same. They think we don't want them with their parents.

There is not much of a back ground given on some of the children before being placed in foster homes. I do believe in time this process will change, or the state agencies will be investigated for not taking their jobs serious. If you remove a child from their home then it's your job to care for that child, like he or she is your own. Not like a commodity, you just separated a family. No matter what condition the child was in that child still and will always want to go back home to their parents. No matter how bad we might think their parent are, as for as their concern, they were in a normal and caring home.

A child's love for their parents runs deep. That child need lots of counseling, as much as possible. After being removed it does something to them. They are not hole anymore. It's like selling a slave to another master. They will never be the same.

Chapter 13

The Creators Expectations

"Life's journey as a free moral agent and the Creator's expectation for ALL is to speak the truth." – Rendra Wilson

The First Step

An unjust man on this earth is the same as a just man

There is no one sin greater than another

Sin is sin

No matter how big or how small

Weakness comes from abuse

Strength comes from overcoming the abuse

The First Steps in overcoming is to admit to being abused

Let's Take Back The Communities.

Proverbs 28:19 He that tilleth his land shall have plenty of bread: but he that followeth after vain persons' shell have poverty enough.

Proverbs 22:6 Train up a child in the way he should go: and when he is old, he will not depart from it.

Proverbs: The rich ruleth over the poor, and the borrower is a servant to the lender.

Let's Worship in Truth, Heal Our Souls and Stop Allowing Others to Teach Us Their Ways.

Matthew 15:9 But in vain they do worship Me, teaching for doctrines the commandments of men.

Matthew 15:24 But he answered and said, I am not sent but unto the lost sheep of the house of Is'ra-el.

Psalms 119:142 Thy righteousness is an everlasting righteousness, and thy law is the truth.

Let's Stay Together as a Family, Father, Mother and Child Our CREATORS First Creation.

Genesis 1: 26,27,28

And God said, let us make man in our Image, after our likenesse: and let them have dominion over the fish of the sea, and over the fowl of the air, and over the cattle, and over all the earth, and over every creeping thing that creepeth upon the earth.
So God created man in His own Image, in the Image of God created He him; male and female created He them.

And God blessed them, and God said unto them, be fruitful, and multiply, and replenish the earth, and subdue it, and have dominion over the fish of the sea, and over the fowl of the air, and over every living thing that moves upon the earth.

Proverbs 14:1 Every wise woman buildeth her house; but the foolish plucketh it down with her hands.

Proverbs 14:16 A wise man feareth, and departeth from evil: but the fool rageth, and is confident.

Proverbs 15:3

"The eyes of the Creator are in every place, beholding the evil and the good."

www.ingramcontent.com/pod-product-compliance
Lightning Source LLC
Chambersburg PA
CBHW070233290526
45789CB00004B/1610